PRAISE FOR *ACE YOUR WAY*

I have tremendous respect for Ben Loeb, who I have known for over 40 years. Ben's record, filled with championships, speaks volumes about his coaching ability—but his resume does not tell the full story about his impact on young people. Most coaches focus on getting the most out of their athletes. Ben challenges his athletes to get the most out of themselves. This perspective makes his book an important read for leaders in all industries!

—JEFF MOORE

author of *Strive Together: Achieve Beyond Expectations in a Results-Obsessed World;* former women's tennis coach, University of Texas; two-time NCAA Division I National Champions (1993 & 1995); NCAA Division I National Coach of the Year, 1993

Coach Ben Loeb joins the brotherhood of Mr. Miyagi (The Karate Kid), Gandalf (Lord of the Rings), and Yoda (Star Wars) as an enlightened guide and mentor. Coach Loeb reminds me of these storied mentors in his empowering book *ACE Your Way*, which provides life lessons, keys, analogies, and vignettes that have served him and others throughout his legendary coaching career. His insight is the template for a life of abundance on and off the tennis court.

—GREG PATTON

former men's tennis coach, University of California - Santa Barbara, University of California - Irvine, and Boise State University; two-time NCAA Division I National Coach of the Year (1987 & 1997); Intercollegiate Tennis Hall of Fame

ACE Your Way is the book for you if you want to succeed in sport and in life! By the time you get to the final page, you will have numerous mental tools in your toolbox to help you move through all that life throws at you. Ben has a way of making seemingly intangible topics—such as focus, confidence, and managing emotions—relatable and simple to integrate into your day to day life. As a mental performance coach, I highly recommend Ben's *ACE Your Way* for athletes and non-athletes, as mental skills are life skills. Just as consistent, daily practice in your sport leads to mastering the physical skill, repetition of these mental tools will allow you to master your thoughts, feelings, and behavior, positively impacting your life as a whole!

—DR. MADELINE BARLOW
mental performance coach; sport psychology coordinator, Drexel University

The best mental game cues are like t-shirts, you'll have to change them often. Coach Ben gets it by serving up *ACE Your Way*. You'll be able to use many of the cues inside of this book as a platform for attacking the challenge ahead.

—DR. ROB BELL
author of *PUKE & RALLY: It's not about the Setback, it's about the Comeback*

ACE Your Way is filled with inspiring stories, anecdotes, and acronyms that illustrate the value of embracing a growth mindset in all aspects of our lives. Ben Loeb, one of the most successful high school tennis coaches in the United States, shares the strategies he's used to enable his teams to thrive both mentally and physically. The multifaceted approaches he applies to help his athletes learn from adversity as well as their accomplishments are also relevant in our everyday lives, as we navigate the challenges and successes that are an integral part of our humanity.

—DR. JOANN HALPERN

director of the Hasso Plattner Institute, New York; adjunct professor in the Department of Applied Statistics, Social Science, and Humanities, New York University

As a very competitive, lifelong recreational tennis player, I couldn't put down Ben Loeb's new book, *ACE Your Way*. I have worked with a personal tennis coach for much of my adult life, and the concepts that Ben relates to real-life are 1) true and 2) adaptive to both games, life and tennis. Tennis requires disciplined focus. Life also requires the ability to focus and remove all other distractions. Adversity and the ability to "reboot" when mired in a temporary losing game is likewise a critical mindset that applies to the game of tennis and to life. Letting go of what we can't control (environmental conditions, a strong opponent) and instead focusing on what we can control (our game, our skill sets, our perseverance) is what makes winners overall. Ben shows us how to accomplish this and more in the book.

—DR. DAVID PHELPS

author of *Own Your Freedom*; founder and CEO of Freedom Founders

Today's athletes must do more than build fitness and refine their technical skills in order to succeed in their chosen sport. Having a strong understanding of how to build and develop your mindset and mental game are just as crucial in the pursuit of becoming your best. In his new book, *ACE Your Way*, Ben Loeb draws on his extensive coaching experience to deliver a comprehensive collection of tools, tips, and concepts that can be applied by anyone in sport and life to help them achieve their goals for success. Ben presents these concepts in a logical, easy to follow format that makes the principles simple to remember and use. I highly recommend this book to anyone wanting to develop an understanding of a high-performance mindset and take their performance to the next level.

—JODII MAGUIRE

founder and director of Think Performance Psychology;
team psychologist, Cairns Taipans, National
Basketball League (Australia & New Zealand)

A·C·E
YOUR WAY

A·C·E
YOUR WAY

100 ACRONYMS, CUE STATEMENTS,
& EQUATIONS TO BETTER
SERVE YOUR LIFE

BEN LOEB, ED.S.

© 2020 Ben Loeb, Ed S.

All rights reserved. No part of this book may be reproduced or used in any manner without the prior written permission of the copyright owner, except for the use of brief quotations in a book review.

To request permissions, contact the publisher.

Printed in the United States of America.
First paperback edition January 2021.

10 9 8 7 6 5 4 3 2 1

Cover and layout design by G Sharp Design, LLC.
www.gsharpmajor.com

ISBN 978-1-7359415-0-9 (paperback)
ISBN 978-1-7359415-1-6 (ebook)

Published by Conversation Publishing.
www.conversationpublishing.com

This book is dedicated to all of the young people I have coached in the sport of tennis—kids from late elementary school through college. The vast majority of the coaching has been with high school tennis teams. We have gone on great journeys together. We have had a lot of success together. But most importantly, we have enriched each other's lives throughout the process. My hope is you have great memories and you learned some things about yourself that will make for a better life.

TABLE OF CONTENTS

INTRODUCTION 1

    1.   **EXCELLENCE** 5

    2.   **FOCUS**............................19

    3.   **CONFIDENCE** 33

    4.   **EMOTIONAL MANAGEMENT** 47

    5.   **FEAR**..............................61

    6.   **ADVERSITY** 75

    7.   **LEADERSHIP** 89

    8.   **TEAMWORK** 103

    9.   **MOTIVATION**...................... 117

    10.   **CHARACTER AND VALUES**........... 131

AFTERWORD: THE GAME BEYOND THE GAME.... 145

ENDNOTES................................. 149

ABOUT THE AUTHOR 151

INTRODUCTION

n. Ace: a person who excels at a particular sport or other activity.

v. Ace: to perform extremely well in something.

AN ACE ISN'T EASY. It's one of the most difficult shots to hit in tennis. When done right, an ace looks effortless—an unreturnable, indefensible serve. But there's effort, alright. An ace takes a lot of practice, through which an athlete pursues excellence by building their game with focus, confidence, character, and emotional management, while dealing with fear, adversity, and motivation. When part of a team, excellence takes leadership and teamwork. This pursuit isn't easy.

As a coach, I've spent most of my life studying the game of tennis and the psychology of sport performance. What I've learned over the many decades is simple: we can develop skills in sports that apply well to the other parts of life.

The trouble is, life is messy. We are bound to struggle, fail, fall down, and feel defeated. We're not always skilled at life. But we can develop our skills and work toward a better life. We just need a few coaching tools to sharpen our game.

That's why I wrote this book. To share with you the coaching tools that have helped me and countless others to do better in sports and life.

ACE stands for Acronyms, Cue Statements, and Equations. These are little mental coaching tools I've used time and again. I put 100 of the best "aces" in this book. My hope is you'll use a few of them in your own life.

This book is written to inspire the reader through their reflection. I say "reflection" because this book is a group of reflections, thoughts, and ideas. The intention is to challenge you to think about how each entry can impact your life. I encourage you to reflect on where you are now, and where you can go, with the reflections that have value to you. As a collection of coaching tools, the purpose of the book is to help you help yourself to become a better version of yourself—one with more joy, confidence, resiliency, self-acceptance, and happiness.

My suggestion is to read one chapter a day, then record your thoughts on how a given reflection or group of reflections can impact your life. Read and reflect on one chapter a day for 10 days. I encourage you to discuss your interpretation of a selected entry or group of entries with someone else. I am hopeful discussions take place between a parent and a child, among friends, teammates, and coaches, and with players, counselors, clients, and more.

The time it takes to read a chapter is short. The time to reflect and respond is dependent on how much you are willing to put into it. The book is the vehicle and you are the driver. Only you can decide how far you are willing to drive with this. Hold yourself accountable to reflect, grow, and re-examine your personal psychological growth. Plan for periodic follow-up review, which is critical to reflection. You can make a difference in your own life and in the life of others in which you have a discussion. "ACE" your way to a deeper and richer meaning in your life!

EXCELLENCE

IS EXCELLENCE DETERMINED by the outcome of a contest, or is it measured by how well you perform? Is excellence about how well you perform relative to a standard set by other athletes, or is it relative to your *own* standard of personal excellence? These are critical questions I've had for teams I have coached.

I suggest you define "excellence" relative to how well you are capable of performing. Of course, it's only natural, and realistic, to compare yourself to others. In any performance, the outcome does matter. For any competitor striving to win, victory is part of why they play the game. For the outcome-obsessive competitor, it might be the only reason they play the game. But in the pursuit of excellence, take a step back and reflect on what you can control.

Is striving for personal excellence something an athlete can control? Yes. The outcome, however, is something you *influence* but not control. Consequently, I challenge you to make it your mission to be the best you can be—to strive for your own standard of excellence.

Several years ago, I spoke with long-time University of Missouri football coach, Gary Pinkel, who was inducted into the Missouri Sports Hall of Fame in November 2019, about his philosophy in preparing his team. He described pursuing team excellence without using the term, telling me that his focus was on preparing his team to get better that day. Coach Pinkel emphasized doing that each day with the ultimate goal of becoming your very best. He did not talk about comparison to other teams; the focus and attention to detail was entirely on what he could control to achieve personal and collective team excellence.

Excellence is a process. What are you doing to prepare to be the best you can be? Achieving personal excellence involves taking your ability and preparing smartly and with purpose, making the right effort on game day, and having the mental and emotional will power to see things through when the outcome is on the line. If you can do that, you have successfully achieved, on a personal level, what you were capable of doing.

Sometimes, doing our best is not good enough to get the outcome we want. It is disappointing for most athletes when they lose. But win or lose, there can still be a sense of satisfaction that you strived to achieve personal excellence. You can still choose to respect and love yourself. This will set you up for greater success in your pursuit of personal excellence.

$E = M * C^2$

EXCELLENCE = MOTIVATION * CONFIDENCE²

It's amazing the impact confidence has in achieving personal excellence. Motivation is a key component.

But the belief in oneself is paramount to genuine achievement.

Do you have the ingredients to achieve personal excellence?

SUCCESS = ABILITY + PREPARATION + EFFORT + WILL[1]

Take your God-given ability, prepare properly, give a strong effort, and have the will power to see it through. That's how you achieve personal success.

You have control over your preparation, effort, and will power.

Use your ability the best you can while you focus on the factors you can control.

STEPS TO SUCCESS

S SELF-RESPECT
U UNWAVERING RESILIENCE
C CONFIDENCE IN YOURSELF
C COMPROMISE WITH OTHERS
E ENGAGING IN THE PROCESS
S STRENGTH *(mental and emotional)*
S SUSTAINED EFFORT

*Your pursuit of personal excellence—
the steps you take to improve—is what
makes you a success, today and always.*

MANY PEOPLE HAVE TALENT, BUT ONLY SOME OF THEM HAVE DISCIPLINED TALENT.

Exhibit self-discipline regularly to bring out the best of your talent.

What obstacles do you need to remove to exhibit deeper self-discipline?

This relates to one of my all-time favorite sayings, popularized by NBA champion Kevin Durant:

"Hard work beats talent when talent fails to work hard."[ii]

FOUR-C YOUR WAY TO A BETTER FUTURE

THE 4 C'S: CONCENTRATION, CONFIDENCE, CONTROL, COMMITMENT

Foresee your way to excellence with proper focus, a belief in yourself, poise, and a sustained commitment— especially when you may not want to. Envision your way from today to being better tomorrow, and then take action.

PLAY WITH PRIDE

P **PERSEVERANCE**

R **RESILIENCE**

I **INTERNAL LOCUS OF CONTROL**
(what you do matters)

D **DEPENDENCE ON YOURSELF**

E **ENTHUSIASM**

Take pride in who you are and what you do in every choice you make.

EXCELLENCE = 1 + 2

1 THE DEMANDED MILE
2 THE UN-DEMANDED MILE

Most everyone is willing to do what is demanded of them.

What are you willing to do that is not demanded of you?

ARE YOU DRIVEN MORE TO COMPARE FAVORABLY WITH OTHERS OR TO LIVE UP TO A STANDARD OF EXCELLENCE?

Bring out the best in yourself, don't just focus on comparing well to the opposition.

Comparing favorably matters, but even better is choosing to make your ultimate opponent your own capabilities.

Focus more on what you can control, which is bringing out the best in yourself.

YOU MUST BE WILLING TO GO TO UNCOMFORTABLE PLACES TO ACHIEVE EXCELLENCE.

The essence of achieving personal excellence is a willingness to mentally, emotionally, and physically put yourself in uncomfortable places. That means testing yourself in ways that foster sincere challenge and growth.

EXCELLENCE INVOLVES CHOOSING ABOVE-THE-LINE BEHAVIORS.

Above-the-line behaviors means doing what is expected of you and more.

Below-the-line behaviors is doing less than what is expected of you.

Stay above the line.

2

FOCUS

WHAT IS IT ABOUT FOCUS that makes it so important in big games? I've coached many teams in high-stakes games where suddenly they get caught up on something irrelevant. In the moments that matter most, why is it so hard to focus on what is relevant?

I think the answer is because the outcome to a big game takes on so much more meaning in each player's mind. If you win, you avoid elimination or secure a championship. If you lose, your season could be over. Consequently, it becomes critical, for a team or an individual, to be able to focus on what's relevant at that moment.

Winning is not what's relevant during the process of competing. Winning is certainly a worthy goal, but if you focus on it while playing the game, you lose sight of what's important now. What's important is staying present-focused on what you can do now.

Many years ago, I had the opportunity to speak with Del Harris, at the time the head coach of the Houston Rockets, after a game in Phoenix. This was back in the days when you could go down to the floor level after a game, possibly even getting a chance to visit with a coach or a player. I asked him about a winning mindset. He told me something I have not forgotten in forty years. He said, "Instead of focusing on winning, focus on the things that create winning."

I had to figure it out from there. What I came to realize is you need to focus on the process. You need to focus on the things you can control during the game. You need to focus on strategy, communication, being present in the moment, competitive spirit, emotional control, and confidence in your ability to excel when you need it most. These are factors that affect one's ability to perform at the peak of your capability. Each improves the chances of getting the outcome you want. And it all starts with proper focus.

RELEVANT CUES – IRRELEVANT CUES = PRIME FOCUS

Get rid of the stuff that doesn't matter. Focus on the things that matter, and the things you can control, in the moment. A "What if I lose?" mentality is the type of stuff that is counter-productive in the now.

FOCUS - FORM AN ARC

A ATTENTION (TO)
R RELEVANT
C CUES

Let the top of the arc symbolize prime focus, the place you want to be.

It's not a peak you strive for, but a plateau you can achieve consistently.

What are your relevant cues?

CTC

C CHANGE
T THE
C CHANNEL

CHANGE YOUR SELF-TALK FOR BETTER PERFORMANCE

You may not be able to control your thoughts, but you can manage your thoughts. Replace negative or counter-productive thoughts with positive thoughts of what you intend to do.

WIN

W **WHAT'S**
I **IMPORTANT**
N **NOW**

Focus on your next move rather than dwell on a missed opportunity, or fret over a potentially negative outcome.

FOCUS ON THE NOW

N NEXT
O OPPORTUNITY
W WAITING

Embrace the next opportunity that awaits you; it's the only opportunity you can influence.

FOCUS ON YOUR ABC'S

A **ACT** *(body language)*

B **BREATHE**
(slow, deep breathing to regroup)

C **CUE WORDS**
(or a short phrase to refocus)

Your body language says a lot about you.

Make it strong. Breathe to relax, and speak to yourself in a constructive way.

THE OUTCOME MATTERS, BUT FOCUS ON THE PROCESS.

Winning matters to a lot of us, but focus on the things you can control along the way.

Your attitude and effort are a good place to start.

FOCUS FOLLOWS FUN.

The joy of competing enables prime focus, and fun sets you free from the psychological chains that bind you.

What do you love most about the game?

PLAY WITH ABANDON

To play with abandon is to play unconcerned about the outcome.

Instead, focus on playing all out.

Little kids teach us this in how they play.

Then we grow up and let stuff get in our way.

This attitude can apply in sport, business, and life.

To perform with abandon allows for a state of flow, of natural focus.

"DON'T THINK TOO MUCH. YOU'LL CREATE A PROBLEM THAT WASN'T EVEN THERE IN THE FIRST PLACE."

—SUKHRAJ S. DHILLON[III]

Sometimes we need to get out of our head.

Thinking too much can lead to ruminating, which means over-thinking a situation.

It can happen on the field of play or while obsessing over a predicament in life.

Reflection can be good, but consider the time, place, and duration.

3

CONFIDENCE

I BELIEVE THE MOST IMPORTANT factor in being able to ACE Your Way to the top of the mountain, is having confidence in your ability to climb. For many people, this is a lot easier said than done, especially when they come up against legitimate resistance in their pursuit of victory. Do you have an inner belief you can achieve great accomplishments when the demands placed upon you feel hard to overcome?

For example, it can be especially difficult to face an opponent you have recently lost to by a sizable margin. When it's time for a rematch, it's so easy to let doubt overcome you. They beat you before—what's to stop defeat from knocking you down again? The same can be true in sports, where they have rankings or times/distances (i.e. track & field; swimming). The comparison game before the contest can lead to negative expectations for some individuals or teams.

Confidence keeps your head up, with the knowledge that you have what it takes.

I remember in 2003, we had an opportunity to see if the unthinkable could happen. Early in the regular season, our high school girls' tennis team lost at home against the team to beat for the state title, by a score of 8-1. Our girls were committed to working hard the rest of the season with the hopes of a rematch in the state Final Four. Working hard is important, but by itself will not maximize your potential. The girls had to accept and embrace the "confidence challenge." Could we see demanding situations as challenges to embrace with enthusiasm and a firm belief we could win?

As the season progressed, we faced significant challenges in some dual meets. The way the team responded to those challenges with a great sense of poise and confidence was a good indicator of things to come. The team made strides in handling pressure situations. The team was also improving their skill set, which added to our growing confidence.

We got the rematch we wanted in the state finals. It was a hard-fought dual meet from beginning to end. The difference-maker was the willingness of our girls to be confident in their success—even when recent history had shown otherwise. We went on to win the dual 5-3 and claim the state championship. It was likely the greatest reversal in state tennis history, from a regular-season loss to winning the state title. It could not have been done without both hard work and confidence.

THE CONFIDENCE CHALLENGE

Are you willing to develop the attitude to see demanding situations as challenges that you embrace with enthusiasm?

MAINTAIN A VIEW OF CONFIDENCE

V **VISUALIZE SUCCESS AND THE DESIRED OUTCOME**

I **INITIATE** *Take the initiative*

E **ENERGIZE** *Turn up the positive energy.*

W **WILL IT** *Show willpower, especially in the clutch.*

Your perspective will create the momentum to achieve great things. Bring the light of confidence, backed by proper preparation, to see your capabilities be rewarded.

YES, I CAN!

Y YEARN FOR THE CHALLENGE
E EMBRACE THE OBSTACLES
S SUPPORT YOURSELF

The safe route is doubt and it's easy to prove yourself right.

The harder route is the conviction that you can.

Doubt Road takes you to a place you don't want to be.

Conviction Highway is the interstate that gives you the opportunity to arrive at your desired destination.

BE BOLD

B **BELIEVE IT** *(Think you can)*

O **OWN IT** *(Take responsibility; be accountable)*

L **LOVE IT** *(Love what you are doing; enjoy the process)*

D **DIVE INTO IT** *(Give it your all)*

Take the risk to be bold in your belief in yourself.

Make someone else, other than yourself, prove you wrong.

What's stopping you from being bold?

BE DATA DRIVEN

D DREAM (HAVE A VISION)
A AND
T TAKE
A ACTION

We all dream about things we want to do or accomplish.

But only some of us take action to make those dreams come true.

HOPE

H HOLD
O ONTO
P POSITIVE
E EXPECTATIONS

Maintain a fighting spirit, resiliency, and the confidence to push through to reach your goals. The ability to stay positive is fuel for confidence.

CONFIDENCE INCREASES WHEN A>D

PERCEIVED ABILITY > DEMANDS PLACED UPON YOU

See yourself as able to overcome the demands of the opposition.

What signs help you see your ability is greater than the demands?

CONFIDENCE CAN BE LIKE A WAVE—IT FLUCTUATES.

Accept the fact that it's normal for confidence to have ebbs and flows. Stay positive and persevere in the face of resistance.

"LIFE ISN'T ABOUT WAITING FOR THE STORM TO PASS. IT'S ABOUT LEARNING HOW TO DANCE IN THE RAIN."[IV]

—VIVIAN GREENE

True confidence comes from dancing in the rain despite any mixed feelings.

You learn to trust in your preparation and yourself, that you are prepared for this moment.

You take decisive action, rather than hope your opponent falters or that your self-doubt would just fade away. You move forward with a conviction that you can do this.

"GO CONFIDENTLY IN THE DIRECTION OF YOUR DREAMS."[V]

—HENRY DAVID THOREAU

My favorite quote of all time. We all have dreams or visions of good things we want to happen in our life. But do we have the genuine confidence and perseverance to pursue them? Without confidence, we may never start.

EMOTIONAL MANAGEMENT

EMOTIONAL MANAGEMENT CAN be a dilemma on and off a playing field. It can be upsetting for athletes when things aren't going well, or when momentum shifts during the game. The same is true for most people off the field of play. It's difficult to maintain your composure when someone challenges your character or is disrespectful to you.

I'll give you a sports example from 2019. I attended a United States Tennis Association sectional tournament in Springfield, MO, which was for the better players in the Missouri Valley section of the USTA.

One particular match was tight between two very good players for their age group, boys 14 & under. The big difference between the players was in how each handled the pressure. One player showed great composure on the court. He constructed points well and showed a lot of emotional resiliency when things did not go his way. The other boy was worth the price of admission if they had one. He was entertaining to watch—that is to watch have a meltdown. Whenever he made a mistake, he would look over at his parents, as if to say, "Help me," or "See, I can't do anything right today." I think at some level he was blaming his parents for his predicament. He was playing the victim role.

Needless to say, the player who maintained his composure and displayed strong competitive spirit ultimately won the match. He looked very comfortable closing it out. Nothing was rushed, yet he applied sustained pressure. Meanwhile, the boy who lost looked distraught, then somewhat relieved when the struggle was finally over.

I am not going to tell you it's easy to manage your emotions all of the time. It can be a challenge for many people, both kids and adults, on and off the field of play. What I suggest is to set a goal for your emotional management. Hold yourself accountable. If you screw up from time to time, maybe your goal is to recalibrate and get back on the right track. Emotional management is a skill, and it requires practice like any other. Hopefully, many of the reflections in this chapter will help you become more skillful at emotional management.

POSITIVE ENERGY

Positive energy is like a muscle.

The more you use it the stronger you get.

COMPETITIVE FIGHT + EMOTIONAL CONTROL = COMPETITIVE BALANCE

Picture yourself on a balance beam with both hands stretched out to maintain your balance. On one hand, you need competitive fight, and on the other hand, you need emotional control. You need both to maintain your balance, mentally and emotionally.

LOOK FOR YOUR OPPORTUNITY IN LIFE

- **O** **OPEN TO SELF-DISCOVERY**
- **P** **PASSIONATE**
- **P** **PERSISTENT**
- **O** **OPPOSITION-READY** *(you can deal with it)*
- **R** **RESPONSIBLE**
- **T** **TRUSTWORTHY** *(establish mutual trust)*
- **U** **UNIFIED** *(respect differences and value things in common)*
- **N** **NOURISHING** *(of your relationships with other people)*
- **I** **INTROSPECTIVE** *(look at yourself honestly)*
- **T** **TRANSFORMATIVE** *(you welcome and handle life's changes, good and bad)*
- **Y** **YOU** *(you count too)*

See each new situation as another opportunity in life for discovery.

ARE YOU CALM IN THE STORM OF COMPETITION?

C CENTERED IN THE HERE AND NOW
A ACCEPTING OF WHAT *IS*
L LOGICAL IN YOUR THINKING
M MINDFUL OF YOUR NEXT MOVE

*Can you maintain a sense of
calmness in the eye of the storm?*

THE 3 Rs FOR COMPOSURE

- R **RECOGNIZE YOU ARE DWELLING ON MISTAKES**
- R **REGROUP BY INTERRUPTING THE CHAIN OF THOUGHT**
- R **REFOCUS ON THE NEXT PLAY**

Ruminating on mistakes is another R, but one you want to avoid. It's good to reflect, but not good to obsess over an issue.

It's easier said than done, but have a game plan to regroup and refocus.

PLAY WITH YOUR HEART

H   **HARD WORK**
E   **EXCELLENCE**
A   **ATTITUDE**
R   **RESILIENCE**
T   **TENACITY**

When you are not sure what to do, think less and trust your heart to lead.

YOU CAN'T AFFORD TO MAJOR IN MINOR PROBLEMS.

We've all heard "Don't sweat the small stuff."

Minor problems are the small stuff that we cannot let consume us. We have the ability to sort out what really matters from what does not.

What minor problems are you majoring in?

SELF-COMPASSION FOSTERS RESILIENCE.

There are times you need to remind yourself you need to be your own best friend. Flip the switch from self-criticism to forgiveness and self-encouragement.

BREAK THE CHAIN!

Break the chain of thought that emotionally holds you back from looking at a situation objectively.

There are times we allow ourselves to get caught up in negative self-talk. Create some space from the struggle by stepping back emotionally to reevaluate, then reframe your view for greater productivity.

"MAINTAIN YOUR COMPOSURE. CONTROL YOUR EMOTIONS. RESPOND, DON'T REACT!"[VI]

—RICK MCGUIRE

Emotional Management is dependent on composure and how you respond. Life on and off the field can get chaotic. Then what?

5

FEAR

FEAR CAN PARALYZE YOU, both on and off the playing field. One product of fear is a feeling of anxiety concerning the outcome of something. We all have fearful experiences, when we've imagined a terrible outcome. I remember one fearful experience I had as a young boy of about eight years old.

I was on the high dive at a swimming pool, trying to get up enough nerve to jump. Jumping off the low dive was easy, something I'd done many times. But psychologically, the high dive put me in a different stratosphere. As I looked down at the water, it seemed so far away. The fear factor kept me on the diving board debating whether to jump or retreat to safer ground. My dad saw my trepidation and said, "Go ahead and jump. I guarantee you will be okay." So, I went ahead and jumped. Sure enough, it was pain-free (no belly-flop or landing on my back), and I was relieved. Wow! Guaranteed success.

That turned out to be one of the last guarantees of that kind. In competitive sports, and most areas of your life, there are no guarantees. There is a level of uncertainty and doubt in which we live, work, and play. In such situations, people can experience a range of emotions, such as confidence, doubt, fear, and many others. Fear can manifest itself in a fear of failure, fear of success, fear of rejection by others, fear of your own self judgment (self-esteem), or even fear of death.

You are introduced to many situations in your life where the outcome matters. When it matters or when there is an inherent danger in a situation, you might have a fear response. My hope is this upcoming chapter will give you some reflection points on how you can better manage fear. A few quick suggestions would be to look at a situation as a challenge instead of as a threat. Ask yourself, "Am I afraid of heights?" I was afraid of heights on the diving board. Learn to adjust to the new altitude in your life, even when you have mixed feelings and no guarantees.

FEAR

F FALSE
E EMOTIONS
A APPEARING
R REAL

You can move from a threat-based "what-if" vision of what you don't want to happen to a challenge-based vision of what you do want to happen.

What FEAR is present in your life today?

ARE YOU AFRAID OF HEIGHTS?

ARE YOU AFRAID OF GETTING BETTER AND THE EXPECTATIONS THAT MAY COME WITH IT?

The higher you climb the ladder of success, the more the altitude can create self-doubt and discomfort.

Allow yourself to become comfortable with your own success with less regard for other people's expectations.

TAKE THE RISK AND GO FOR IT

R RESPOND TO THE CHALLENGE
I TAKE THE INITIATIVE!
S SUBMERGE YOURSELF IN THE BATTLE
K BE KIND BY USING AN UNEMOTIONAL EVALUATION

The hardest part about "diving" off the higher platform of uncertainty is taking action despite your reservations.

You may need to believe in your preparation, visualize success, trust, and go.

EAT A PEAR

CAN'T HANDLE THE PRESSURE? TO STOP THE CHOKING, EAT A "PEAR"

P PRESENT-FOCUSED

E ENERGY MANAGEMENT IN YOUR MIND AND BODY

A AX THE NEGATIVE

R REFOCUS WITH A POSITIVE PERFORMANCE CUE

Performing in high-pressure situations is so much harder than in non-pressure situations. Learn to embrace high-pressure situations with positive energy while ridding yourself of negative self-talk.

GO FAR IN LIFE MANAGING FEAR

F BE FREE TO EXPLORE THE UNKNOWN
A ACCEPT THE CHALLENGE
R BE RESILIENT

Freedom to explore the unknown starts with being okay with yourself. This allows you to better manage accepting risk in your life.

ALWAYS A-TACC THE BULL'S EYE

A

T TANK

A ANGER

C CHOKE

C CHALLENGE

You may experience tanking (withdrawing effort), anger (getting upset), or choking (getting very nervous) as emotional reactions in the competitive arena. But this serves as an opportunity for self-discovery to guide you to the ultimate goal of finding the center of the target, which is seeing the situation as a challenge.

FEAR OF FAILURE + FEAR OF SUCCESS = FEAR OF SELF

If you fear failure or fear success you fear the pressure it creates inside of you. Self-acceptance and self-discovery will enable you to move beyond the fear. What do you need to accept and discover about yourself?

FAITH

F FULLY
A ANTICIPATE
I IT
T TO
H HAPPEN

Believe it will happen.

Then set yourself free to trust yourself and go.

If someone is going to prove you wrong, it should not be you!

Discover the possibilities without self-doubt undermining your intentions.

"I THINK I KNOW MY PATTERN: I SET MYSELF UP FOR FAILURE BECAUSE THAT'S SOMETHING I'M USED TO. I KNOW I CAN SUCCEED, BUT UNLESS I GET HELP, I WON'T BE ABLE TO."

—A FORMER STUDENT AT ROCK BRIDGE HIGH SCHOOL; COLUMBIA, MO

Some people feel uncomfortable leaving their comfort zone of mediocrity. It's easier to stay mediocre than to excel. See yourself as being comfortable with success. And remember, asking for help is a strength, not a weakness. There's no need to appear invulnerable.

"A LOT OF PEOPLE ARE AFRAID OF COMMITMENT BECAUSE IT MEANS THEY'LL HAVE TO SAY, 'THAT'S THE BEST I CAN DO.' THEY ELECT TO BE AVERAGE. WHEN YOU COMPETE, YOU DECIDE TO FIND OUT WHAT YOUR REAL LIMITS ARE, NOT JUST WHAT YOU THINK THEY ARE."[VII]

—**PAT SUMMIT,** *Hall of Fame Women's Basketball Coach, University of Tennessee*

Courage is the willingness to take risks, regardless of the possibility of failure.

ADVERSITY

"When the Blues go marching in,

Oh when the Blues go marching in.

Oh Lord, I want to be in that number,

When the Blues go marching in."

I SANG THAT SONG FOR fifty-one years. That's how long the St. Louis Blues were in the NHL going into the 2018-2019 season, having never won the Stanley Cup. As I've gotten older, I have told people in all seriousness, "I want to see the Blues win the Stanley Cup before I die." If the Chicago Cubs could go more than a century without winning the World Series, could the Blues suffer the same fate?

When the teams I've coached in high school tennis have won the state championship, I have referred to it as like winning the Stanley Cup. It's so special and such an amazing feeling to invest, commit, dream, and accomplish something of such great magnitude together, especially when it means so much to you. It would be a similar emotional experience if my beloved St. Louis Blues won the Stanley Cup.

There was one big problem during their 52nd season of 2018-2019. The Blues were in last place in the NHL on the morning of January 3. The team had faced a lot of adversity, endured tough losses, a coaching change, and at times, poor play. I thought they would be better off losing and getting a higher draft pick — build for season #53.

The odds of making the playoffs, let alone winning the championship, were not good. No professional sports team had been in last place at that point in their season and come back to win the championship. But that is exactly what they did. The team had tenacity, a strong belief, and amazing resilience after losses. They faced adversity and kept going. There were many teams in the league that had talent as good as or better than the Blues, but no team developed heart, chemistry, and resolve beyond that of the St. Louis Blues. Against the odds, the Blues did go marching in and win the Cup!

Besides inspirational team stories, there have also been many athletes that have come back from significant injuries and returned to top form. It takes a lot of perseverance to overcome physical setbacks. But what about overcoming a setback in mental health?

Michael Phelps, arguably the greatest swimmer of all time, has had an ongoing battle with depression and anxiety. It's hard to fathom being your best, let alone the best in the world, when you are fighting depression. Mental health issues are another form of adversity that everyday people face on and off the playing field. Michael was humble enough to seek help, but it's he who deserves the credit for dealing with these obstacles. Michael Phelps won 23 gold medals and 28 total medals in his Olympic swimming career between 2004-2016 — the most of any athlete in Olympic history. He did it by facing adversity in and out of the pool.

See yourself as being able to rise above the chains that bind you. Use the success of teams or other people as inspiration. You, too, can overcome adversity in your life to achieve success and, more importantly, find happiness.

ADVERSITY = LEARNING OPPORTUNITY + GROWTH OPPORTUNITY

Adversity creates an opportunity to learn something about yourself and to grow from it.

The key is to look at adversity as an opportunity to test yourself. See adversity as a challenge and embrace it.

HANDLE ADVERSITY BY PLAYING ABOVE THE RIM

R REFLECT ON WHAT HAPPENED
I IMAGINE THE WAY YOU WANTED IT TO BE
M MOVE ON

"Rebound" from adversity through reflection, then envision the change you seek. The hardest part of dealing with adversity is to "Move On."

Even when you care deeply, you need to allow yourself to get to a better mental and emotional place.

ELMO

E ENOUGH,
L LET'S
M MOVE
O ON

It's normal to reflect on an issue or a defeat in your life, but don't obsess over it.

Find acceptance and then move on.

EFFORT

LET YOUR ...

E ENERGY
F FLOW
F FREELY
O ON THE
R RIVER
T TODAY

Life is like a flowing river where time keeps moving.

Rather than let your energy get stuck on the rocks (obstacles), let it flow.

Find a way to get around them.

POUR YOUR HEART & SOUL INTO IT

P POWER
O ON (WITH)
U UNLIMITED
R RESERVES

You leave yourself emotionally vulnerable when you invest so deeply. Show your inner strength to power on, no matter what.

FIND MEANING IN DEALING WITH ADVERSITY:

Ask yourself,

"What emotional muscle am I strengthening today?"

VULNERABILITY + COMPOSURE + PERSPECTIVE = ADVERSITY MANAGEMENT

Accept your vulnerability.

Have the composure to deal with it.

Is your perspective a view primarily rooted in emotion or objectivity?

How do you manage your own vulnerability to overcome adversity?

REBOOT YOUR COMPUTER
BE RESILIENT

When things are not going right with your computer you might decide to reboot it. Take a re-centering breath or two to clear your mind of clutter, then begin again with a fresh outlook.

YOU CREATE ADVERSITY AND ANXIETY WHEN YOU BELIEVE THE DEMANDS ARE GREATER THAN YOUR RESOURCES.

Adversity can come from what someone else is doing, or it can come from your restrictive beliefs about dealing with a situation. See overcoming adversity as part of the challenge. Eliminate the part that is self-imposed.

"MISTAKES ARE A FACT OF LIFE. IT IS THE RESPONSE TO THE ERROR THAT COUNTS."[VIII]

—NIKKI GIOVANNI

Everyone makes mistakes. It's how you process the errors that matters most.

Do you let mistakes consume you?

Do you let mistakes become a global view of your inadequacies as a person?

Or can you see mistakes objectively, and then show the resilience necessary to move on with what to do next?

LEADERSHIP

LEADERSHIP CAN BE MULTI-DIRECTIONAL, as in leading yourself and others. Do you have the self-discipline, self-motivation, and self-confidence to lead yourself on a path to success and happiness? To be a good leader starts with the self. If that is where it ends, so be it. You will accomplish a lot in life.

Being in a leadership role is not for everyone. It can be a tough gig. Some people are cut out for it, others are not. However, those that are in leadership positions do have the opportunity to learn and grow on the job.

Back in the late 1980s, a tennis coach in the Big 8 conference (now Big 12) commented to me on the success of another coach, and he said something I'll never forget about leadership and a person being able to change. He said in a six-month period, you can make significant changes in your approach for the better. Today, we would call that a "growth mindset." Major change starts within you before it starts with other people. For example, how you deal with criticism or others second-guessing you: you need to figuratively carry a shield to deflect criticism. It takes real strength to do this without getting defensive.

The coach that allegedly changed his approach

went on to have a very successful career as the head women's tennis coach at the University of Texas. His name is Jeff Moore. His teams won the NCAA Championships in 1993 and 1995 and reached the finals in 1992 and 2005. He is now a well-respected authority on leadership, and the author of the excellent book, *Strive Together*.

One of my favorite personal stories happened in the early 1990s when I reached out to meet the head football coach from my undergrad alma mater, the University of Colorado. The University of Colorado played at the University of Missouri in Columbia, MO. I wanted to meet the CU head football coach, Bill McCartney, because he was a man of high moral character, a person with firm convictions, a strong leader, and a very successful football coach. The main reason I wanted to meet him was to talk to him about leadership.

I went to the visiting team's hotel and hung around long enough to meet Coach McCartney coming out of a meeting room. I explained I was a CU grad and that I was now living in Columbia teaching high school and coaching high school tennis. I don't remember my exact question, but I do remember the specific answer he gave me nearly thirty years ago about his philosophy on leadership. He said, "some people will appreciate what you do for them *now*, some in a few years, and some will never know." The critical part of this statement is the power of the last few words. I interpret it to mean that some people will never appreciate what you are doing for them, now or ever. A strong leader has the inner strength to be okay with themselves, no matter how people view them. Strength of conviction! Not easy to do, preventing those doubters and disbelievers from penetrating your armor. The more durable their inner strength, the more successful a leader.

BE A GREAT LEADER OF YOURSELF & OTHERS

L **LONG-TERM HORIZON** *(a vision for your journey)*

E **EXPECTATIONS FOR WHAT YOU WANT TO ACCOMPLISH**

A **ACTION** *(act boldly)*

D **DURABLE** *(manage the resistance)*

E **ENGAGEMENT IN THE JOURNEY WITH POSITIVE ENERGY**

R **RELATIONSHIP-BUILDING DURING THE PROCESS**

Leaders build relationships, take action, and engage in the process for the journey.

ACT LIKE A LEADER

- **A** **ACTION-ORIENTED**
- **C** **CONTROLLING OF YOUR EMOTIONS**
- **T** **TEAMWORK-FOCUSED** *(promote working together toward team goals)*

There are times a leader can feel vulnerable.

Lead anyway.

CALF ROPE YOUR WAY TO SUCCESS!

C COMMUNICATE OPENLY AND HONESTLY

A ASPIRE TO MANAGE STRESS WELL

L LEAD YOURSELF AND OTHERS IN A CONSTRUCTIVE DIRECTION

F FOCUS ON THE THINGS YOU CAN CONTROL

The first step to sustained success is to have open and honest dialog among players and coaches, teachers and students, parents and kids.

OWN THE STANDARDS OR CONFORM TO RULES

What does it mean to own the standards? It means going beyond following the rules—it means abiding by the accepted norms of behavior and proudly upholding them for the team.

There will be greater buy-in with accepted, reasonable standards versus forced, inflexible rules.

LEADERS THAT LAST…DON'T LET THE RESISTANCE STOP THEM!

It's impossible to please all the people all of the time.

Good leaders understand that.

Listen but lead.

THE *10 + 10 + 80 = 100* EQUATION*

A typical group is made up of...

> *10 percent who help the leader lead in an effective direction;*
>
> *10 percent who lead in an ineffective direction with their agenda;*
>
> *80 percent who decide which leadership group to follow.*
>
> **Exact numbers vary based on the group.*

The leaders of the team need to get the 80 percent group to follow them. The remaining 10 percent may surrender.

GREAT LEADERS...

- **SET A HIGH STANDARD**
- **LEAD BY EXAMPLE**
- **EXHIBIT CONFIDENCE**

  Show confidence in yourself when encountering resistance from others.

  Show confidence in others when they experience self-doubt.

EFFECTIVE LEADERSHIP STARTS WITH TAKING CONTROL OF YOUR OWN LIFE

Take an inside-out approach.

Manage yourself to better manage others.

"PEOPLE SEE THAT YOU PUT A LOT INTO IT AND PUSH THEM TO BE BETTER. SOME MAY NOT APPRECIATE IT AT THE TIME, BUT THEY WILL LOOK BACK AND SAY 'YOU WERE THE BEST COACH I'VE EVER HAD.'"

—**ERIN BUCKO,** *a senior student-athlete at Rock Bridge High School, Columbia, MO. Oct. 25, 2006.*

GREAT LEADERS EMPOWER OTHERS.

The goal of a leader is to empower others to become self-reliant. Whether you are a parent, a coach, or a manager, you should teach the people you lead to become less dependent on you, and more dependent on themselves. This will lead to more happiness and confidence in life.

8

TEAMWORK

TEAMWORK IS A VITAL PART of a team's success. This does not mean everyone needs to be best friends and spend a lot of time together away from the team or work facilities, but it does mean that team members want to work together, compete together, and strive together to achieve common goals. Teamwork means you value each other for what each team member brings to the group. It also means you value each other as people, and you show respect for one another. The best way I can sum up what I have tried to instill in the teams I coach is to "Embrace the Journey... Together." I even have a coaching cap with that inscription. I want to remind the kids I coach that embracing the journey we go on during the season is a valuable part of the experience. If we embrace it together, we will be more enriched, and we stand to perform better as well.

There is a team in professional sports that I became a big fan of a few years ago because I think they chose to embrace that philosophy, and I admired them greatly for their unselfish play. That team is the Golden State Warriors of 2015 thru 2019. The Warriors had many outstanding individual players, but their coach, Steve Kerr, got them to put their ego aside for the betterment of the group.

The Golden State Warriors had Steph Curry, Klay Thompson, Draymond Green & Co. from the beginning of their run in 2015. They won the NBA Championship in 2015. In 2016, they lost in the finals, due in part to a questionable suspension of a key player. But the coach and the team made no public excuses. I distinctly remember Coach Steve Kerr mentioning what I think is one of the hardest lessons to learn in life: you give it your best shot and then you have to move on. This is part of the challenge of adversity. Do you have the mindset to play above the RIM (Reflect back, Imagine forward, Move on)?

The Warriors added Kevin Durant before the start of the 2015-2016 season. There is only one basketball and the Warriors knew there was a greater mission than individual accomplishments. Kevin liked the team's culture, and he fit right in, helping the team win the NBA Championship in both 2017 and 2018. In 2019, the Warriors made it to the finals for the 5th consecutive year, but injuries to Durant and Thompson were too much to overcome in the finals.

The Warriors won and lost with class during this five-year run. The thing that all of us can learn from it is the value of teamwork. There is value in taking whatever talent you have, working cooperatively and competitively with other people, and striving together to reach common goals.

TAKE A TRIP GO ON AN ADVENTURE TOGETHER

T TEAMWORK
R RESPECT
I INTENT
P POISE

Each season is a journey together.

Make the TRIP an adventure filled with the purposeful intent to bond and achieve together. Strive to win together, but also strive to bond together.

ARE YOU WILLING TO CARE ALONG THE JOURNEY?

C **COMMITMENT** *...do what it takes to achieve personal and team excellence*

A **ACCOUNTABILITY** *...for your effort, performance, and results*

R **RESPECT** *...of your teammates, coaches, opponents, self*

E **ENTHUSIASM** *...by showing a positive attitude with the team and within yourself*

You may not know where the journey will take you, but you do have control over how much you CARE.

TEAM

T TOGETHER
E EVERYONE
A ACHIEVES
M MORE

There is no greater feeling than accomplishing with others.

Invest together
Grow together
Rise and fall together.

RESPECT IS THE KEY TO TEAMWORK

R REFLECT ON HOW YOU TREAT OTHERS AND YOURSELF.

E EVERYONE COUNTS, SO SUPPORT EACH OTHER.

S SINCERITY—BE GENUINE IN ALL THAT YOU SAY AND DO.

P PARTICIPATE, DON'T JUST FOLLOW.

E ENCOURAGE OTHERS AND YOURSELF.

C CONNECT WITH OTHERS.

T TRUST EACH OTHER.

Respect is the most important element in establishing a thriving team culture.

DEFINE YOUR TEAM PURPOSE TO BRING CLARITY TO YOUR TEAM MISSION.

Purpose—why we do what we do

Mission—what we want to accomplish

*For a personal perspective,
replace "we" with "you."*

OPEN COMMUNICATION + COMMON EXPECTATIONS + COLLECTIVE IDENTITY = TEAM COHESION

Team Cohesion works best when you have open communication among members, common expectations, and a collective identity to show what you are all about. Describe your collective identity.

THE ABCs OF DEVELOPING AN EFFECTIVE TEAM CULTURE

A ATMOSPHERE *(team environment)*

B BEHAVIOR *(acceptable norms of behavior)*

C COMMUNICATION *(how you will interact with each other and deal with conflict)*

Effective team culture will have a safety net in place to deal with differences of opinion when they arise. The team should establish and understand the ABCs. It will sustain an effective and positive team culture.

FEEDBACK: ARE YOU OPEN OR ARE YOU CLOSED?

Be open to feedback whether you agree with it or not.

Respond in a non-defensive manner.

Listen openly, don't "reload" your response while receiving feedback.

NO PRIZE WON FOR YOURSELF CAN COMPARE TO THE GREAT FEELING OF ACCOMPLISHMENT AND PRIDE SHARED BY A TEAM AFTER A BIG VICTORY.

Winning together is the ultimate feeling of accomplishment. The preparing together, sacrificing together, dreaming together, and experiencing ups and downs together make the biggest victories that much more meaningful.

"ANYTHING CAN HAPPEN AS LONG AS THEY *TRUST* THEMSELVES, TRUST EACH OTHER, *BELIEVE* IN THEMSELVES, AND BELIEVE IN EACH OTHER."[IX]

—JAIME ASHWORTH,
Duke Women's Tennis Coach February 12, 2014

The operative words here are "trust" and "believe." For teamwork to take place on a team, in a marriage, with close friends, or in the workplace, there must be trust and belief in one another to sustain a happy and productive co-existence. When it's not there, communicate in a cooperative way until it is.

MOTIVATION

THE ROOT WORD OF "MOTIVATION" is "motive," which is the root cause of an action, or the underlying reason *why* you do something.

Motivation is the foundation for all accomplishments. It is the driving force behind other mental factors in achievement like commitment, perseverance, focus, confidence, and managing your emotions. An athlete, student, spouse, and employee all need the driving force of motivation to achieve meaningful accomplishments.

Motivation comes in two forms extrinsic motivation and intrinsic motivation.

Extrinsic motivation comes from factors outside of yourself such as rewards, like winning the championship trophy, a medal, publicity, and attention from others.

Intrinsic motivation comes from inside of yourself, like pride in your accomplishments, self-satisfaction from personal improvement, or simply the thrill of competing. There is nothing wrong with valuing both forms of motivation. However, it's longer-lasting and typically more meaningful if the primary source of motivation is intrinsic.

I remember when our high school boys' tennis

team was seeking its fourth consecutive team state title in the spring of 2019. We were trying to achieve a 4-peat for the five seniors that were varsity starters for all four years. That would be quite a feat. As a coach, I had to emphasize intrinsic motivating factors (i. e. pride in accomplishment) over the extrinsic factors (i. e. notoriety from the accomplishment). The same could be true for our girls' team that was seeking to win its fifth consecutive team championship in the fall of 2018. If accomplished, that would tie the all-time state record for consecutive championships.

I emphasized process over outcome during the season. We had to find motivation in things we could control, like striving together for collective excellence, rather than the magnitude of the feat. Fortunately, both teams won their respective championships, which was extremely gratifying.

Winning can make it easier to feel motivated in sports and in life. It's easier to put the time, effort, and energy into something when things are going well. However, for some people, losing, or a lack of progress, can also become a motivating force to invest at a higher level in order to attain better results.

If you don't get the promotion, the win, the respect, or the recognition for an accomplishment, you have to decide if you will emotionally and physically withdraw, or if you will become energized to do something about it.

It's easier to be motivated when things are going well. The ultimate test of your will — your drive — is to find motivation when things are not going your way.

If you are a coach or a parent, try this motivational tip: the strongest form of motivation is *encouragement*. Start with that in your efforts to motivate others, but you can also apply it to yourself. We are often our own worst critics; being too hard on yourself can be a losing game. Consequently, use self-encouragement to inspire yourself. Sometimes, you need to be your own best friend. I hope you find the reflective thoughts in this chapter of value to you, both on and off the playing field.

INTRINSIC MOTIVATION > EXTRINSIC MOTIVATION

THE MOTIVATION FROM WITHIN YOU SHOULD BE GREATER THAN THE MOTIVATION FROM OUTSIDE YOU.

Pride experienced from accomplishment should be of greater value than the reward or publicity from the accomplishment. Intrinsic motivation lasts longer.

PERFECTIONISM IS AN ILLUSION. BEING HARD ON YOURSELF IS A LOSING GAME.

Too much self-criticism will make it more difficult, not less, to perform well when you are in a similar situation the next time. The same holds true for happiness in life.

"THE BEST WAY OUT IS ALWAYS THROUGH."[X]

—ROBERT FROST

Show the courage to dive into a predicament in spite of your reservations about how it will turn out. Learn to embrace a predicament wholeheartedly, with inquiry and a desire to change things for the better.

LOOK AT A SITUATION AS A CHALLENGE, NOT AS A THREAT.

A challenge seeking mindset leads toward achievement, while a threat mindset increases the chance of failure.

SET SMART GOALS

S SPECIFIC
M MEASURABLE
A ATTAINABLE
R RELEVANT
T TIME-BOUND

Record goals and then set up a schedule to monitor the progress of reaching your goals.

KEEP SAIL-ING

S SUCCESSIVE
A ATTEMPTS
I IN
L LEARNING

Be a striver in your determination to keep sailing along against any headwinds.

EMBRACE THE JOURNEY

Many people are consumed by the outcome.

Value the opportunity to go on a great journey regardless of the outcome.

MEANINGFUL ACCOMPLISHMENT IS MOVING FROM WHAT IS TO WHAT COULD BE.

Be determined and energized to move from the way things are now to what could be.

THE STRONGEST FORM OF MOTIVATION IS ENCOURAGEMENT.

There is negative feedback, positive feedback, and no feedback.

The type of feedback you give to others and to yourself is your choice.

There are times you need to treat yourself as your own best friend.

Which type of feedback is more likely to get you to the place you want to be?

"ENERGY FLOWS WHERE INTENTION GOES; CREATE YOUR DAY."[XI]

—KALINDI DINOFFER;
Virtual Tennis Symposium 7/14/20

Your intentions can become very powerful.

*Intentions set the tone for the day
no matter your circumstances.*

*They give you a direction to
answer questions such as:*

*What do you want to do?
Who is the person you want to become?*

10

CHARACTER AND VALUES

A PERSON'S CHARACTER AND VALUES will influence how successful and happy they will be in sports and life. Think of character as ethical standards and core values as a person's beliefs. Both character and values will mold how a person will handle the ups and the downs of life. Character is indicative of personal integrity. Integrity is staying true to doing what is right, regardless of the situation. The part I *value* most about exhibiting strength in character is a willingness to stand up for personal principles. This is not easy because you may face resistance. Be honest with yourself and others. Listen, grow, and adapt, as you face the world that will at times test your character.

On the teams I have coached, the #1 value I want us to live by is respect. I have taught a sport psychology course for 9 years. The #1 value in team dynamics the students mention in their writings is respect. Respect is a common denominator between players and coaches, students and teachers, as well as managers and supervisors, in a properly functioning team environment or personal relationship. It's also paramount in the relationship you have with yourself! This is why respect is the first value listed in the character equation in this chapter.

Some task-oriented examples of important values include dedication, responsibility, confidence, and resiliency. Other import personal values include humility, compassion, love, and self-acceptance.

Two athletes immediately come to my mind--athletes whom I hold in such high esteem for the character and values they exhibit on a regular basis. One of them is Roger Federer, world-renowned tennis player. Many people have great admiration for what he has accomplished in his tennis career. To date, he has won 20 grand slam titles and over 100 tournaments on the professional tour. But what I admire most about Roger is the type of person he is. He is humble, kind, classy, and such a great sportsperson. Roger continues to play on the pro tour at age 38 because he loves the game. He does not worry about what will supposedly happen to his legacy if he loses to younger players. He plays anyway because he still loves the challenge of competing. Additionally, he is very philanthropic, making many donations to the education of underprivileged kids around the world.

Another of my favorite athletes who leads his life with such class and dignity is Russell Wilson, the quarterback of the Seattle Seahawks. Wilson shows great leadership and enthusiasm on the field no matter the situation. But what impresses me so much about Wilson is his ability to be fiercely competitive on the field, yet so gracious after the game. He also supports many great causes through his charitable giving foundation. Russell has joined the Banfield Foundation's Safer Together initiative in an effort to provide more resources to pet owners in abusive situations.

I also want to share with you the personal values mentioned in the book, *Win the Day*, by Jerry Lynch; foreword by Steve Kerr. How many of these personal values do you exhibit in your daily life? Character (doing the right thing); Compassion; Commitment; Courageousness; Gratefulness; Integrity; Joyfulness; Respectfulness; Selflessness (self-sacrifice for the betterment of others); Vulnerability (willingness to share imperfections or concerns about self).

My intention is for you to be inspired by these examples and the role models in your life, and hold yourself to a standard of being true to yourself. I hope the reflective thoughts from this chapter can provide further inspiration as well.

RESPECT + INTEGRITY + DEDICATION = CHARACTER

Respect for others and yourself

Integrity in your honesty and ethical qualities

Dedication to being committed to a task

WHAT YOU DO WHEN NO ONE ELSE IS LOOKING ARE THE THINGS THAT HELP DEFINE YOU.

It's easy to do the right thing when someone is watching you.

But what defines you more is what you do when no one else is watching and you won't receive credit.

HONOR

H   **HUMILITY**
O   **OPPORTUNITY TO SERVE OTHERS**
N   **NOBILITY** *(high moral principles)*
O   **OPEN IN COMMUNICATION**
R   **RESPECTFUL**

It's your choice whether or not to live your life with honor.

ENTER THE RED ZONE OF SUCCESSFUL CORE VALUES

YOU CAN CHOOSE TO BE...

R **RESILIENT**—*show the ability to power through and bounce back from adversity*

E **ENGAGED**—*bring your full focus to the endeavor*

D **DETERMINED**—*strive for your goals in a positive way*

GREAT AMERICAN VALUES ARE INSTILLED IN WHO YOU ARE…

Freedom   *to choose what you want to make of your life*

Pride   *in what you have become because of your efforts and accomplishments*

Opportunity   *to seek challenges in your life of your choosing*

WHICH VALUES DO YOU SEE IN THE MIRROR?

Self-reflect and then share with someone else. See if you demonstrate:

RESPECT **INTEGRITY** **COMPASSION**

DEDICATION **CONFIDENCE** **RESPONSIBILITY**

NEVER ABANDON YOURSELF.

Never abandon your self-image of being worthy.

You are worthy no matter if you win or lose, the color of your skin, your gender, religion, sexuality, or the amount of money you have. You are worthy unconditionally.

LIFE IS NOT A GAME OF PERFECT

Find acceptance in your imperfections yet strive to become the person you are capable of becoming.

More importantly, discover internal peace and happiness.

WAIT

W WHY
A AM
I I
T TALKING?[XII]

— **DONNA ZAJONC,** *Master Certified Coach*

Most people listen with the intent to reply, rather than with the intent to understand.

Value the willingness to truly listen to what the other person is saying before formulating a reply.

"LET US SEIZE THE OPPORTUNITY TO DISCOVER A NEW CARING, ONE GROUNDED IN A NEW AWARENESS, NEW COMPASSION, AND NEW EMPATHY. WE CAN START BY MAKING A HEARTFELT COMMITMENT TO TREAT ALL PEOPLE EQUALLY AND WITH THE RESPECT THEY DESERVE."[XIII]

—PETE CARROLL,
Seattle Seahawks Football Coach, referencing the public response to the death of George Floyd (May 25, 2020).

AFTERWORD: THE GAME BEYOND THE GAME

HAVE YOU HEARD THE EXPRESSION, "Good things don't last forever, but good people do"?

Some examples of that could be your high school experience; playing on a high school sports team; being part of the high school band, school plays, choir, or your college experience; etc. I remember hearing my college experience would be the best days of my life. Bummer! Do you mean the top of the happiness inverted-U-curve would be at the end of my college years? Your life goes downhill upon graduation? If so, no wonder some people try and play an encore by stretching out undergrad for five years or go to grad school.

It's human nature to want to stay in your comfort zone. Why change a good thing? As for leaving college for the workforce, many people do not want to enter the "Responsibility Invite Tournament" for the next 40-plus years of their life. Staying with the tournament sports analogy reference, it's hard for many people, myself included, to have your best sports days behind you. You used to be better than that, but not now. The high school, college, or pro athlete might find themselves transitioning from a competitive athlete on a team to becoming a semi-competitive individual athlete, a recreational participant, or an exerciser at the gym.

The point is, *life happens!* Things change. You are who you are, you are not what you do.

Be careful of the self-identity and/or self-esteem trap where you see your worth tied directly to how well you perform compared to others. For instance, "I am a swimmer." That's who I am. Compare this to the perspective of "I am a person who swims competitively."

The "game beyond the game" is whether or not you are able to separate what you do in an actual game (i.e. tennis match) or at a station of life (i.e. well-liked and recognized in high school; "he's a cool dude"), from who you are as a person? Do you find peace and happiness within you? Do you find happiness from being you?

There is nothing wrong with striving to win in sports, business, or at any stage of life. It only becomes a problem if you tie your overall self-worth and happiness to a particular outcome. The more you care, the more vulnerable you are to the ups and downs of life. But care anyway! Have confidence in yourself that you are a resilient person. Look in the mirror daily and tell yourself you are resilient and worthy if you doubt it. Then take action and live it. Life will have its disappointments, joys, failures, and successes. Dealing with the lows is easier when you have the attitude you will get to a better place. Life will have its changes, many of which are good. Cherish good memories, but focus on embracing the challenges, the opportunities, living with contentment on the road ahead.

Set new goals as you transition through life. Goals are best if they are written down and reviewed periodically. Goals may have to do with exercise, work, relationships, meditation, personal growth, and more. Remind yourself of your goals as motivation during challenging times as well as when things are going well. My hope is the content in this book will inspire you to reflect on how to live a good life. There is value in the game but more value in the game beyond the game.

Best wishes on your journey through life.

ENDNOTES

i   Rick McGuire; Ben Loeb; Amber Selking; Patrick Ivey, Mental Toughness: *The Athlete's Playbook: Building a Culture of Mental Toughness: The Pyramid Model.* (Championship Productions, 2020). (Author has made changes to the formula as it appeared in original source)

ii "Kevin Durant - Player Page: Oklahoma City Thunder," NBA.com, Accessed August 24, 2020, https://www.nba.com/thunder/team/kevin_durant.html.

iii Sukhraj S. Dhillon, *In Search of God: The God of Spirituality* (CreateSpace Independent Publishing Platform, 2011).

iv Vivian Greene, "Leadership: Dance in the Rain," *The Journal of Healthcare Contracting*, August 25, 2020, https://www.jhconline.com/leadership-dance-in-the-rain.html.

v   Henry David Thoreau, *Walden and Resistance to Civil Government: Authoritative Texts, Thoreau's Journal, Reviews, and Essays in Criticism* (New York: Norton, 1992), Chapter 18 (paraphrased).

vi Rick McGuire, "Foundations of Positive Coaching," Missouri Institute for Positive Coaching, Accessed August 22, 2020, https://education.missouri.edu/positivecoaching.

vii Laanna Carrasco, "Coaching Legend Pat Summit: Summing up the life of the NCAA's winningest coach," *Basketball for Coaches*, June, 2016, https://www.basketballforcoaches.com/wp-content/uploads/2016/06/Pat-Summitt-Bigger-Faster-Stronger.pdf

viii Nikki Giovanni, "Of Liberation," *Oxford Essential Quotations* (4 ed), (Oxford University Press, 2016).

ix   Jaime Ashworth, email to Ben Loeb, February 12, 2014.

x   Robert Frost, *North of Boston*, (New York: Henry Holt and Company, 1915).

xi   Kalindi Dinoffer, "Mindfulness for Parents, Players and Coaches," Tennis Coaching Clinic video, Accessed October 19, 2020, https://tennis.coachesclinic.com/talks/mindfulness-for-parents-players-and-coaches.

xii David Emerald, "W.A.I.T. Why Am I Talking?" TED Video, Accessed October 19, 2020, https://tennis.coachesclinic.com/talks/mindfulness-for-parents-players-and-coaches.

xiii Pete Carroll, "Let us seize the opportunity to discover a new caring..." Facebook, June 3, 2020, https://www.facebook.com/coachpetecarroll/photos/a.116655668370168/2996455863723453/?type=3.

ABOUT THE AUTHOR

BEN LOEB has done extensive research in the area of sport psychology, self-improvement, and team building. He is the author of two published books. His first book, *Next Level Coaching: How to Use Sport Psychology to Educate, Motivate, and Improve Student-Athlete Performance,* was published in 2018 (Greenleaf Book Group). The second book he co-authored which is entitled, *The Athlete's Playbook Building a Culture of Mental Toughness: The Pyramid Model*, was published in 2020 (Championship Productions).

Ben developed a curriculum guide for a course in Sport & Performance Psychology. He has taught the course at Rock Bridge High School in Columbia, Missouri, for nine years, where he also coaches both the boys' and girls' tennis teams. The teams he has coached have won 1,138 dual meets (tied for most wins in Missouri state high school history, as of year-end 2020), nineteen state championships, and forty-one Final Four appearances (20 boys, 21 girls) in his thirty-two years as a high school tennis coach.

Before coaching at Rock Bridge High School, Ben coached at Hickman High School in Columbia. He also coached the women's tennis team at the University of Missouri–Columbia while achieving an Educational Specialist degree from the College of Education (1988).

Ben has coached in many United States Tennis Association sectional and national team events. He has also applied sport psychology concepts with his teams for 35 years. He has received many coaching achievement honors, including awards from the United States Professional Tennis Association, the Missouri Sports Hall of Fame, the Kiwanis Club of Columbia, the *Columbia Tribune*, and the National Federation of State High School Associations at both the state and the sectional level.

> *Want more Ben?*
> *ben@benloebcoaching.com*
> *https://benloebcoaching.com*

www.ingramcontent.com/pod-product-compliance
Lightning Source LLC
Chambersburg PA
CBHW040420100526
44589CB00021B/2764